Jordan

Images from the Air

Jordan

Images from the Air

Jane Taylor

Al-'Uzza

BOOKS

Foreword

From the hills to the desert to the sea; from ancient ruins, to modern urban streets, to gleaming domes and minarets – the aerial eye is a witness, not only to Jordan's tremendous variety, but to the deep connections that bind us as a people and a nation. This is the vision that Jane Taylor offers in her new collection of aerial photographs: the record of a landscape that is both God's and man's, historic and modern, eternal and dynamic.

Jane Taylor's extraordinary photographs are more than works of art. They are a testament to the author's deep understanding of Jordan and the many dimensions of our society. First is what we might call the "vertical" dimension: the hearts we lift up to God. In these pages, the photographer's lens captures, again and again, the central role of faith in the cultures and communities of Jordan. For us, from ancient times to the present, the Divine has always been close. It is a spirit that inspires our national values and drives our search for peace.

A second dimension is "horizontal" – the land to which we belong, our home and our anchor in a global century. Jane Taylor's artistry captures the tremendous range of Jordan's environments and seasons. This includes spectacular natural heritage areas and historic sites. It also includes a rich array of community life, from urban centers to rural highlands, badia communities, market towns, the port of Aqaba, and Jordan Valley farms. These communities reflect Jordan's history as a center for global interactions – a movement and mixing of people and ideas, which is the foundation for our belief in cooperation and tolerance.

Another aspect of Jordan that these photographs capture so well is the dimension of time. Ancient archeological remains, some of them thousands of years old, testify to a vast, uninterrupted human presence on this land. But Jordan's heritage is not frozen in the past. The continuity of our society has had a profound impact on contemporary Jordan's proud sense of heritage and our commitment to a future of achievement.

As one who has often experienced the awe of seeing my country from the skies, I am delighted to help introduce Jane Taylor's new book. In the pages that follow, readers can travel with her to experience a new vision of our remarkable country. I hope that those who already know and love Jordan will discover in these pages new perspectives on its wonders. For those who are new to our country, these pages are an exceptional opportunity to meet the people, heritage and spirit of our land.

'Abdullah bin Al Hussein

Page 1:
Storm clouds over evaporation pools
at the southern end of the Dead Sea

Pages 2-3:
Mountains near Dana on a hazy day

Page 6:
Part of the vast area of southern
Jordan known as Wadi Ramm

Pages 8-9:
Karak's 12th-C Crusader castle in
1985, before repairs were made to the
glacis and walls

Published in 2005 by Al-'Uzza Books
PO Box 831313, Amman 11183, Jordan

Text and photographs copyright
© Jane Taylor, 2005

Jordan National Library Deposit No:
1622/7/2005

ISBN 9957-451-06-5

Designed and typeset by
Andrea El-Akshar, Köln

Printed and bound at the National Press,
the Hashemite Kingdom of Jordan.

Exclusive distribution in Jordan by
Mazen al-Haris
PO Box 10051
Amman 11151
Tel: (+962 6) 464 3139
fax: (+962 6) 477 6954
mobile: 079 554 2905

Contents

Dedicated to the memory of
HM King Hussein of Jordan

Preface

'Why Jordan?' people kept asking. It was 1978 and I was about to go there on holiday. We all knew it was in the Middle East; most knew of King Hussein; some volunteered that it harboured a magical place called Petra; a few had heard of Jarash; one or two had been there. The general consensus was that it consisted mainly of desert and had no seasons – it was hot, dry, monochrome and dull.

How wrong we all were. My first visit was in autumn, with sun-filled days that were pleasantly warm; later I found clear, cold winter weather (or rain, or occasionally snow), the sharp greenness of spring, and summers of perfectly tolerable dry heat.

I shared the astonishment of 19th-century western travellers at Jordan's breathtaking natural beauty and variety. And, as if the work of Nature were not enough, for the past few thousand years human beings have strewn these landscapes with awe-inspiring monuments.

Amazed to find no books that portrayed its grandeur, I set out to record this little known treasure in words and photographs. This book is part of that quest, an attempt to share some of the enormous privilege I have had in my bird's eye view, which started just twenty years ago.

⊰❧

In the autumn of 1985, on one of my by now frequent visits to Jordan, I tentatively asked the then Secretary-General of the Ministry of Tourism, Nasri Atalla, if it were possible to do some aerial photography. I had envisaged hiring a small high-winged plane, as I had

The Treasury at Petra, seen from above the end of the Siq
Right: A waterfall in a remote wadi

10

done elsewhere, but I quickly understood from him that in those days only military helicopters were available.

'But let's ask', he said, adding that I should not automatically expect a positive result from his request on my behalf to the Royal Jordanian Air Force. Indeed I expected nothing, but a few days later I was asked to come for a meeting with the commander of No. 7 Squadron, and to bring a list of the sites I had in mind.

For one full day and two half-days I sat in a military helicopter with my feet dangling a few hundred metres above those spectacular and varied landscapes that I had so far seen only from the ground. Jordan's millions of years of geology unrolled beneath me — its deserts and dramatic gorges, fertile plains like patchwork quilts, granite mountains which dissolved into exotic sandstone formations and transformed again into smooth limestone hills. And scattered casually amid this glory were grand reminders of thousands of years of human civilisation. I was utterly captivated.

The result was my first Jordan book, *High Above Jordan*, published in 1989. Since then, and having made Jordan my home, I have been able to do yet more aerial photography with the RJAF, sometimes for new book projects of my own, at other times sitting in (with cameras) on other people's sorties. From above I have seen vast land formations in a single glance, or a lone migrating stork over the Dead Sea. I have noted the creeping growth of towns and villages, the remoulded profile of archaeological sites (particularly Petra) as they were excavated, the care lavished on some ancient monuments and the unhindered decline of others.

A Super Puma helicopter of the Royal Jordanian Air Force flying above Wadi al-Mujib

Left: Rolling farmland near Petra in the last light of the day

Much of Jordan's terrain has great visual drama and excitement — the wild sandstone mountains in the south, palm trees growing out of the side of a sheer limestone cliff further north, a waterfall in a remote wadi. But it can also produce moments of unexpected tranquillity — an olive grove crowning a hill, a flock of sheep following the shepherd home in the evening... There are delightful anachronisms too — in a valley between pre-Cambrian granite mountains, a modern diesel train transports its cargo of phosphates to the port at Aqaba; or, in desolate desert, sheep and goats drink from a Roman reservoir.

Once, with bedouin friends from Petra, I floated in surreal silence above the vastness of Wadi Ramm, in one of a fleet of hot air balloons competing for the Champion of Champions crown. Punctuating the sky above these aeons-old geological formations were not only brilliantly coloured balloons in conventional shapes, but others in the guise of a champagne cork, a whisky bottle, two jumbo jets, a turreted castle and a Smurf. Awed by the grandeur of the mountains, our pilot admitted that his normal business of flying champagne trips over Californian vineyards paled by comparison — Ramm was as 'vast and echoing and godlike' for him as it had been for T. E. Lawrence.

When I started work on this book in early 2004, I knew there were still gaps in my coverage of Jordan's sites — some I had never photographed, others were so altered by years of excavation that new photographs were needed. Thanks to the renewed generosity of the RJAF, I was able to fly on a crystalline March day in 2004.

A diesel train taking phosphates to Aqaba for export

Right: Hot-air balloons float above the splendour of Wadi Ramm

We started with the grand hilltop fort of Machaerus (the cover picture), glowing in the first rays of morning sun and set off to perfection by the sapphire backdrop of the Dead Sea. On we sped through an unmarred and golden day and, as we skimmed over emerald fields of growing wheat, grey-green olive trees grounded in rich red earth and rugged beige mountains lightly touched with a veil of spring grass, I photographed a range of sites dating from prehistory to the present.

But as I worked on the text and looked more closely at the photographs I identified more problems, caused not only by tireless archaeology but also by urban development. Aqaba, for example, had metamorphosed since I had last photographed it from the air in 1998 — new hotels and houses, a marina and the tallest flagpole in the world had transformed Jordan's only seaport. I had to do more photography.

Then I was told of a tiny two-seater bubble of a plane called Seeker, developed by Seabird

A flock of sheep makes its way home in the evening along a path between olive orchards

Aviation Jordan (part of the King Abdullah Design and Development Bureau), which is now building these aircraft under licence from Australia for commercial and security surveillance purposes. It is excellent to photograph from – its high wings, and the engine, are behind the cockpit, thus giving exceptional visibility; it is considerably more economical on fuel than a helicopter; and for a fixed-wing aircraft it is unusually manoeuvrable. The directors were open-hearted, the pilot rejoiced in a new challenge, and I and my cameras were airborne again.

While the vehicle was perfect, other things did not always go smoothly. One morning a few early clouds decided to have some fun, multiplying rapidly and swallowing up the sky as we neared Jarash. After a few despairing circuits we gave up and made for Pella, as the western sky

looked clear — we could take in Jarash again on the homeward run. The clouds obligingly stayed away at Pella and Umm Qays, both dressed in their spring-green clothes. But the ancient gods of Jarash had a final trick up their sleeves — as we flew in for the second time, the clouds swept into position once more.

Not all the gods had been unkind. There had been one short burst of sunshine glory during our first attempt and, when the films returned from the processors, two photographs (one is on pp. 50-51) had caught that moment. They eased the loss of almost everything else.

This book contains photographs taken at various times in the past two decades, and in different seasons. Spring is short and glorious and most of my recent photographs present this abundant face of Jordan. But the landscapes of summer, autumn and winter have their own drama and beauty, painted with a rich palette of every shade of ochre and brown, showing more clearly the contours of the earth, the plan of a classical city or the intended shape of an ancient building. I have come to love these brown landscapes every bit as much as the green.

Above: The Seeker surveillance plane

Right: The basilica terrace at Gadara (Umm Qays), with the Ottoman village to the left

18

Acknowledgements

My foremost thanks are to HM King 'Abdullah bin al-Hussein for so generously contributing the Foreword to this book. I am also grateful to HM Queen Rania al-'Abdullah for her interest in my work; and to HRH Prince Faisal bin al-Hussein, who facilitated my flight in March 2004. In addition, I wish to thank HRH Princess Muna al-Hussein and TRH Prince Ra'ad bin Zeid and Princess Majda Ra'ad for perennial kindnesses.

This distillation of twenty years of aerial photography in Jordan has been made possible by the multifaceted generosity of many people, starting with HM the late King Hussein, who encouraged my early work and contributed Forewords to my first two Jordan books; and HM Queen Noor, who brought my work to King Hussein's attention.

The Royal Jordanian Air Force has been both generous and highly professional in all my sorties. With their policy of anonymity, I cannot name the pilots who rose cheerfully at unspeakable hours in the morning and seemed to know in their bones how to set up a good photograph – all I had to do was release the shutter. My heartfelt appreciation, admiration and thanks to them all.

My most recent sorties (in the Seeker surveillance plane, with Seabird Aviation Jordan) were thanks in particular to Alec Mackenzie, Gilles Latour, John Schofield and Omar al-Massarwah; and to Seeker's irrepressible and excellent pilot, Muwaffaq al-Khalaylah.

The Ministry of Tourism and the Jordan Tourism Board have always been supportive; so too has the Department of Antiquities, in particular its present and past directors, Dr Fawwaz Khraysheh and Dr Ghazi Bisheh, and also Dr Fawzi Zayadine – to the last two, and to Dr Piotr Bienkowski of the Manchester Museum, I am grateful for having read the whole text and made vital corrections, suggestions and additions. I am also indebted to Dr Ignacio Arce for information about his work at Qasr al-Hallabat, which is rewriting the story of that site. If I have clung to any misconceptions, the fault is all mine.

Particular thanks are due to Sara Mengüç and Lesley Aylwin, both luminaries of books in their different ways, for their invaluable editorial help; and to Judith Eagle for picking up inconsistencies and typographical errors in the text.

My 16 years (so far) of living in Jordan have been made a delight by the friendship, hospitality and encouragement of so many friends, both Jordanians and other westerners who have made Jordan their home – in particular Mamdouh & Basma Bisharat, Flavia Romero, Patricia Salti, Aysar Akrawi & Adnan Habboo, Isam & Nihad Ghattas, Tamam & Abdul Rahim Jalal, the late Ruth & Moraiwid Tell, Na'ila & Samir Jabaji, Hisham & Maha Khatib, Marie-Claire Marroum, Isabelle Ruben, Hana Sadeq, Suzi Nasir and her parents Janette & the late Raji Nasir, Fa'eq & Dua'a Haddad, Salah & Fatma Khleifat. A special thank you to Omar Sukhon who kept my computer alive in

Left: A migrating stork flies south in autumn over the Dead Sea

21

A 127-metre high flagpole flies the Jordanian flag on the outskirts of 'Amman

Amman, and to my nephew, Matthew Taylor, for doing the same in London.

In Petra, my second home, I have received boundless hospitality and help from dear friends: Dakhilallah Qublan & Rakhiyya, Marguerite van Geldermalsen & the late Mohammad Abdullah, Awadh Salameh, Khalid Dakhilallah, Haroun Dakhilallah & Lidia Jimenez – and many more whose names do not appear here but whose friendship I cherish.

It is always a pleasure to work with two special friends: Andrea El-Akshar, a gifted book designer who combines her German meticulousness with Arab flexibility; and Tom Paradise, Professor of Geosciences and spare-time cartographer, cook and Renaissance man, who contributed the overlay for the map. The base-map (from *High Above Jordan*) is reproduced by kindness of Nick Jones of Lion Hudson Ltd.

Photographic note

Apart from the photographs of 1985 (when I used Kodak Ektachrome 100) all the photographs in the book have been taken with Fujichrome Velvia or Fujichrome Provia. My cameras are a Pentax 6x7 for medium format, and Nikon FE and FE2 for 35mm, the latter only relatively recently superseded by Nikon F100. I have not yet gone digital.

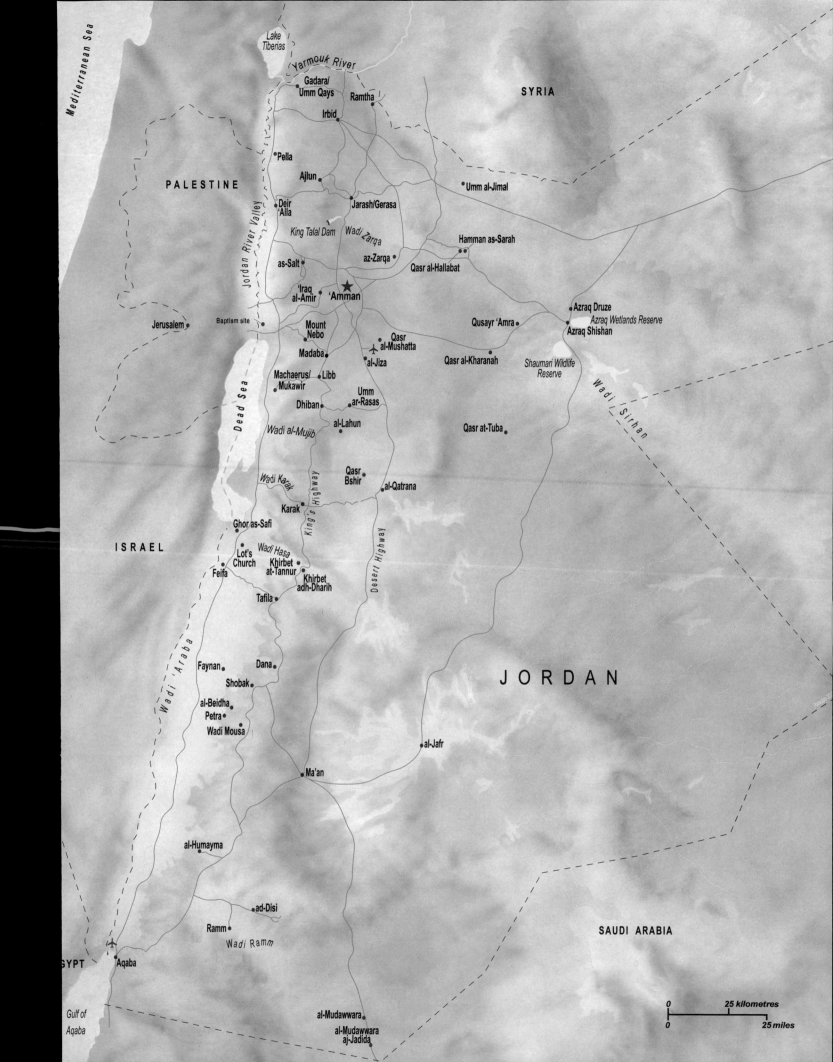

Part 1
In and around 'Amman

'Amman

Few places show the evolution of Jordan's story as clearly as 'Amman, for here we can still see, layer upon layer, many stages in the city's metamorphosis. Once capital of the Iron Age kingdom of Ammon, it became in turn a Hellenistic, Roman and Byzantine city, then heart of the Umayyad province of al-Balqa', an abandoned field of ruins and a late-19th century Ottoman village. It is today capital of the Hashemite Kingdom of Jordan.

The first settlements were on the citadel hill, and were supplied with water from vast reservoirs cut in the rock. Rabbath Ammon, or Rabbah, is first mentioned in the Bible as the place where the huge iron bedstead of Og King of Bashan was brought as spoils of war (Deut. 3). Later, when King David's armies attacked its water supply (2 Sam. 12:27), Uriah the Hittite was sent to die in the front line so that David could marry his beautiful widow, Bathsheba. In the early 6th century BC prophecies by Jeremiah (49:2) and Ezekiel (21:2; 25:3-5) of Rabbah's destruction by Nebuchadnezzar of Babylon may not have been precisely fulfilled but, like the whole region, Ammon became a province first of the Babylonian empire, then of the Persian.

In the Hellenistic period, with the Middle East divided between Alexander the Great's warring successors, the city changed hands periodically between the Egyptian Ptolemies and the Syrian Seleucids, and was rebuilt by Ptolemy II Philadelphus (283-246 BC) who renamed it Philadelphia. The Nabataeans also ruled it for some time.

Prosperity grew under the Romans as a city of the Decapolis, resulting in many new buildings – a theatre, odeon and forum in the lower town, which were connected by a monumental stairway to the new temples on the citadel above. Philadelphia remained wealthy throughout the Byzantine period, when it was the seat of a bishopric, and also after the Arab conquest of 636, witnessed by the remains of a handsome 8th-century Umayyad palace and administrative complex. It is from this period onwards that the city reverted to a version of its early Semitic name: 'Amman.

Decline set in after the Abbasids moved the centre of the Islamic world from Damascus to Baghdad in the middle of the 8th century, and by the 15th century 'Amman was an abandoned ruin. So it remained until 1878, when the Ottomans settled a group of Circassians here who had fled persecution in Russia because of their Islamic faith. It remained small (in 1918 T. E. Lawrence called it a 'village') and only after the Amir 'Abdullah made 'Amman his capital in 1921 did it begin to grow again, expanding from one steep hill to another in a creeping development of pale honey-coloured stone, or concrete. In 1946 the Emirate of Transjordan became a kingdom with 'Amman as its capital, the seat of government and the commercial, legal and administrative centre of the Hashemite Kingdom of Jordan.

Previous pages: Modern 'Amman cityscape

Right: North end of 'Amman's Citadel hill; the vast ancient water cistern is beneath the 8th-C Umayyad palace (foreground) and in front are remains of Bronze and Iron Age walls

The Citadel

The L-shaped citadel hill, inhabited at least since the Early Bronze Age, was fortified at various times thereafter, including massive walls of the Middle Bronze Age. These have recently been excavated on the south-east side of the hill (front right of picture). Apart from this, there are only scant architectural remains from these early times – most of what we see today is from the Roman, Byzantine or Umayyad periods, whose monuments overlie what was there before.

The most significant Roman structure, the temple of Hercules (front left), was built, according to an inscription, when Geminius Marcianus was governor of the Province of Arabia (AD 162-166), and was dedicated to the co-emperors Marcus Aurelius and Lucius Verus. It was not the first sanctuary on this site – remains have been found of an Iron Age shrine, probably dedicated to the Ammonite god Milcom; and the great exposed rock at the heart of the temple of Hercules is thought to have been part of an even earlier sanctuary.

Stones and columns from the temple were re-used in the 5th/6th-century church that lies north-east of it, built to serve the spiritual needs of the small Christian community that remained on the citadel as part of a residential and industrial complex.

In the Umayyad period Roman building material was again re-used to create a palace and administrative offices in what may have been a second Roman temple precinct. It was the headquarters of the provincial governor, appointed by the Umayyad Caliphs in Damascus. Still standing to its full height (though recently restored with a wooden dome), is the monumental entrance hall, a grand waiting room for those wishing to see the governor. Between this and the only modern building on the citadel (the Archaeological Museum) lie the remains of the Umayyad mosque, while to the west of the hall is the large circular cistern which supplied the palace with water.

Above: The L-shaped citadel hill seen from the south, with the temple of Hercules on the left and remains of Bronze Age walls on the right

The Roman theatre

The most imposing monument of Roman Philadelphia, and the best preserved, is the theatre – according to an inscription it was built in the reign of Antoninus Pius (AD 138-61) to hold 6,000 people. The theatre and odeon (which held c. 500) were on two sides of a colonnaded forum, dated 189, of which only part remains. These originally stood beside a stream and a major road, the Decumanus Maximus – the stream is now in an underground culvert and the road has long since been built over. The propylaeum (a triple-arched gate that once stood north of the forum, beyond the stream and road) has also disappeared; it was the entrance to the processional stairway up to the citadel and was mentioned by travellers as late as 1911.

Jabal Jofeh, the hill into which the theatre is built, became the main residential area for the affluent in the early years of the Emirate of Transjordan, in the 1920s and early 30s; but that role soon transferred to Jabal 'Amman and is now held by the area of Abdoun, further to the west.

In 1948 the theatre and ancient tombs along the hillside here provided a first safe haven for some 50,000 Palestinian refugees fleeing their homes in what became Israel. Within two weeks 'Amman's population nearly doubled. Many remained, as citizens of Jordan, and were enabled gradually to replace their tents with the more permanent structures that today stack almost one on top of another on the steep slopes.

Right: 'Amman's Roman theatre, odeon and forum

Following pages: The blue-domed King 'Abdullah I mosque in 'Amman, side by side with the Coptic church

'Iraq al-Amir

In the 5th century BC Nehemiah, governor of the Persian province of Judaea, referred frequently to 'Tobiah, the Ammonite', governor of the province east of the Dead Sea. Two centuries later, in the long conflict between the Ptolemies and the Seleucids, the Tobiah family reappears in the archive of Zenon, an agent of Ptolemy II Philadelphus. In one document, dated 12 May 259 BC and addressed to Ptolemy himself, Tobiah offers a gift of horses, camels, dogs, wild asses and slave boys from his country estate in a well-watered valley west of 'Amman, at today's 'Iraq al-Amir (caves of the prince).

According to the historian Josephus, in his account of events between 190 and 175 BC, Hyrcanus, grandson of the Tobiah of the Zenon letters, built 'a strong fortress... of white marble to the very roof, and had beasts of a gigantic size carved on it, and he enclosed it with a wide and deep moat...'.

The magnificent remains of Hyrcanus' unfinished mansion, Qasr al-'Abd (palace of the [royal] servant), now stand encircled by cultivated land where once the waters of the moat would have mirrored the walls. The dam is still visible at the south-western end. The family's Ptolemaic links were a liability when the new Seleucid king, Antiochus IV, began to extend his kingdom southwards around 168 BC. To avoid a worse fate, Hyrcanus 'slew himself with his own hand; and Antiochus seized all his substance'.

The 2nd-C BC Qasr al-'Abd, once surrounded by a lake, whose dam is still visible bottom right

34

Mount Nebo

Known locally as Siyagha, Mount Nebo is the highest point in this part of the ancient kingdom of Moab. On a clear day there is a magnificent panoramic view over the Dead Sea and the Jordan Valley to the hills on the other side of the rift, with the towers of Jerusalem visible on the skyline.

The hilltop is identified as the place from which Moses looked out over the promised land of Canaan which God had forbidden him to enter; and here, it is said, he died and was buried (Deut. 32:49; 34:1-6). Rather more dubiously, a reference in the apocryphal book of Maccabees suggests that Mount Nebo was the final resting place of the Ark of the Covenant (2 Macc. 2:2-8).

Around AD 384 Egeria, an intrepid lady from an unnamed part of western Europe, visited Mount Nebo in the course of an extensive Christian pilgrimage, and wrote an account of it in her journal. Travelling from Jerusalem on a donkey, she crossed the Jordan River and then climbed this hill, mostly riding though she had to scramble up the steeper parts on foot. At the summit she found a church, 'not a very big one', cared for by some 'holy men' who assured her that 'Holy Moses was buried here', and that 'this tradition came from their predecessors'.

Less than 100 years later another pilgrim, Peter the Iberian, Bishop of Gaza, wrote of 'a venerable and very large temple' with 'many monasteries' around it — but archaeological evidence suggests it was the same church that Egeria saw, the difference in size merely a matter of perception.

The ruins at Siyagha were visited in 1864 by the French Duc de Luynes, whose description of them in his *Voyage d'exploration à la Mer Morte, à Pétra et sur la rive gauche du Jourdain* encouraged more travellers to follow in his footsteps. Interest in the site increased still further after the discovery in 1886 of Egeria's journal, and its publication in the following year; this was followed in 1895 by the rediscovery of the biography of Peter the Iberian. As a result of this interest, in 1932 the Franciscan Custody of the Holy Land purchased the site of Mount Nebo, and under their auspices archaeological investigation began a year later.

Excavations have uncovered a cluster of monastic buildings surrounding a 6th-century basilica which had been enlarged in the 7th century. Within the church are remains of a 4th-century chapel (probably that seen by Egeria and Peter the Iberian), adapted from an earlier structure which may have been a mausoleum. The site appears to have been abandoned in the 9th century.

Since 1976, under the direction of Father Michele Piccirillo, several more mosaics have been found, in particular a magnificent and very large pavement dating to the 6th century with vivid representations both of people and animals — its extraordinarily good state of preservation can doubtless be attributed to the fact that it had lain buried for centuries beneath a later mosaic.

The Memorial of Moses on a hilltop overlooking the Dead Sea, the Jordan Valley and the hills beyond

Madaba

The rambling modern face of Madaba, situated some 30km south of 'Amman, belies the fact that it is the site of a very ancient settlement, which occupied a tell (an artificial mound), which stands out above the surrounding fertile plains.

Referred to in the Bible as Medeba in its account of Moses and the Exodus (Num. 21:30; Josh. 13:9), Madaba was a Moabite town near the borders of Ammon, which tended to change hands from time to time when captured by the Amorites or Israelites. It was one of several towns mentioned in the Mesha stele, or Moabite stone (see p. 99), which recorded the achievements of Mesha, king of Moab in the mid-9th century BC. It tells of his recapture of Madaba (and other places) from the Israelites and its rebuilding. Later Madaba became part of the Nabataean kingdom and, after the 106 AD Roman annexation, it was a thriving provincial town in the Province of Arabia, adorned with fine buildings, temples and colonnaded streets.

Christianity took strong root in Madaba, which became an episcopal see – in 451 its bishop took part in the Ecumenical Council of the church at Chalcedon. In this period, and particularly in the 6th century, Madaba was the centre of a mosaic school, which accounts for the large number of mosaics that were lavished on its churches and public and private buildings. Though the designs emanated from Constantinople, the quality of execution

The excavation area on Madaba's ancient tell, with the Catholic church on the hill above

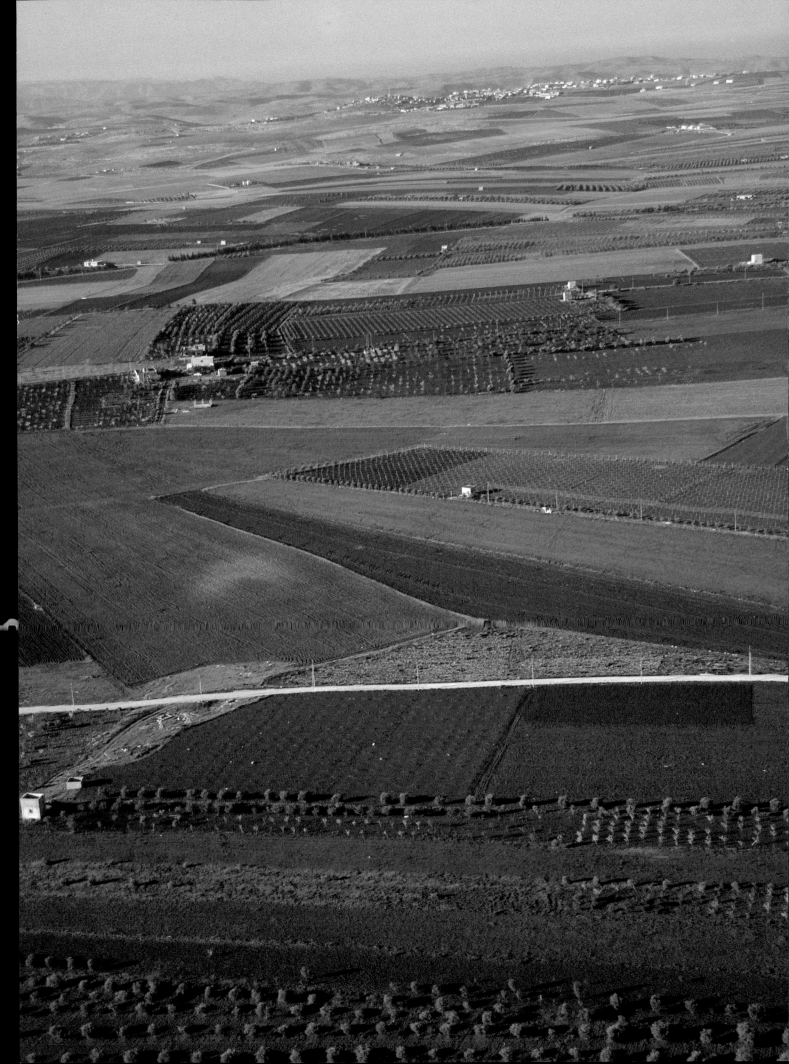

of mosaics in the area is from the skill of the Madaba craftsmen.

Madaba remained prosperous under the Umayyads, and Christians continued to worship in their churches. Decline appears to have set in after the great earthquake of 749 and the defeat of the Umayyads in the following year. From the Mamluk period the town stood abandoned for many centuries – several 19th-century European travellers reported it as a field of ruins surrounded by fertile plains, parts of which were cultivated by local bedouin of the Bani Sakhr tribe.

So it remained until 1881 when three Christian tribes, who had left Karak after a dispute with other tribes, settled among the ruins. Their cultivation of the surrounding farmland inevitably created tensions with the Bani Sakhr who wanted a share of the crops. But with the support of both the Greek Orthodox and Catholic churches, and also of

Madaba's Greek Orthodox church of St George (right) and the shelter of the Archaeological Park (bottom left) in the heart of the town

Left: The fertile plains surrounding Madaba, the patchwork-quilt effect broken by a farm road

the Ottoman authorities, and in some cases with compensation being paid to the bedouin, the settlers were soon allowed to grow their wheat and barley, herd their sheep and goats, and live in peace with their new neighbours. The population is now a mixture of both Christian and Muslim.

It was these 1881 settlers who, in the course of building a new village among the ancient ruins, found mosaics buried beneath the rubble and incorporated many of them into their new houses and churches. The most famous is the unique (but now partial) map of the Holy Land in the Greek Orthodox Church of St George.

41

Machaerus/Mukawir

The local name for this hilltop — *al-mish-tnaqa*, the gallows — carries resonances of its early notoriety, for the fort that crowns it is traditionally associated with the imprisonment and execution of John the Baptist. Dramatically situated in the hills south-west of Madaba, and overlooking the Dead Sea, the fortress of Machaerus lies near the small village of Mukawir, whose name reflects the ancient one. But the story of Machaerus is older than that of John the Baptist.

An earlier fortress was built here by the Hasmonaean ruler Alexander Jannaeus (103-76 BC) to defend his eastern territory of Peraea against the expansionist Nabataeans. So impregnable was it thought to be that Jannaeus' widow and heir, Alexandra, stored her treasure here. But the site proved not to be inviolable — in 57 BC, ten years after Alexandra's death, when the region had descended into civil war between her two sons, the Romans asserted control and seized this strategic fortress, virtually demolishing it in the process. To seal the fate of the Hasmonaean dynasty, in 37 BC the Roman senate proclaimed Herod (later called 'the Great') king over the people and lands of his Hasmonaean predecessors.

Machaerus was rebuilt by Herod both as a palatial and secure summer residence and also as a defence against the neighbouring Nabataeans.

Right: The hilltop palace-fortress of Machaerus, and the Roman assault ramp on the right

Following pages: Remains of the ramp and a number of Roman forts can be seen in patches of early-morning sunlight near Machaerus

According to the contemporary historian Josephus, Herod 'built a wall round the very summit and erected towers at the corners, each 90 feet high. In the middle of this enclosure he built a palace, breathtaking in size and beauty'.

On Herod's death, when his kingdom was divided between his three surviving sons, this area fell to Herod Antipas. Some 30 years later Antipas divorced his wife (a Nabataean princess, daughter of Aretas IV) to marry Herodias, wife of his brother Philip. His rejected wife made her way to Machaerus, then across the nearby border with Nabataea and from there, under the protection of the Nabataean army, she went south to her father's capital at Petra.

John the Baptist, who had so outspokenly condemned Antipas' divorce and remarriage, also came to Machaerus — but as a prisoner. Josephus tells us that it was here that Herodias' daughter Salome danced and, at the instigation of her mother, demanded the Baptist's head on a charger.

When Herod Antipas died, his lands were taken by the Romans who installed a contingent of soldiers at Machaerus. But in AD 66, in the early stages of the first Jewish Revolt against Roman rule, a group of rebels seized the fortress from its Roman garrison. Their respite was brief — soon after the fall of Jerusalem in AD 70, the governor of Judaea, Lucilius Bassus, led an assault against the castle and destroyed it. The forts which the Romans built for the siege, and the ramp they made for the final assault, can still be seen on the ridge below. But the ramp was never used as the defenders surrendered.

The Hill of Elijah and Baptism site

The 'Pilgrim of Bordeaux', in AD 333 the first known Christian pilgrim in the Holy Land, wrote of seeing 'the place where our Lord was baptized by John, and above the far bank at the same place is the hillock from which Elijah was taken up to heaven'.

The prophet Elijah hid from King Ahab in Wadi Cherith, where ravens brought him food twice daily, 'and he drank from the wadi' (1 Ki. 17:5-6). Wadi Kharar in the Jordan Valley, with its spring, has been tentatively identified with Wadi Cherith, and a small hill nearby has for centuries been called Tell Mar Elias (the mound of Saint Elijah), commemorating his ascent to heaven in a whirlwind, with 'a chariot of fire and horses of fire' (2 Ki. 2:11).

St John's Gospel refers to 'Bethany beyond Jordan, where John was baptizing' (John 1:28), and to Jesus going 'across the Jordan to the place where John had been baptizing' (John 10:40). This has recently been identified with a site just east of the Jordan and a few kilometres north of the Dead Sea. It lies near the western end of Wadi Kharar, near the river; the spring there could have supplied both Elijah and John the Baptist.

In the late 5th century a church was built here beside the old course of the Jordan. But the recurrent flooding of the river meant that it had to be rebuilt several times — at least three other churches have been discovered, built in the 6th and 7th centuries.

Elijah's Hill (centre right) and Wadi Kharar; the Baptism site is near where the wadi runs into the Jordan

46

As-Salt

Until the early 1920s as-Salt was the only town of any real significance in Jordan. Thanks to its good water supply and agricultural land, it had been settled at least since the Iron Age. It has been identified with Roman Gadaron; and in the Byzantine period it had its own bishop. Its name (Latin: *saltus* means wooded valley) is said to be the origin of the word 'sultana', from the famed sweetness of the local grapes.

In 1220 the Ayyubid Sultan al-Malik al-Mu'azzam built a fort on the ancient citadel hill, using earlier foundations. Destroyed by the Mongols in 1260, it was quickly rebuilt by the Mamluk Sultan Baybars. After the 1516 Ottoman takeover, when as-Salt became the regional capital, trade with Palestine brought increased wealth. The fort was destroyed again in 1840 by Ibrahim Pasha, and 30 years later was replaced by the Ottomans with a barracks. It is now the site of a large mosque.

As-Salt's greatest prosperity was in the late 19th century when wealthy Nablus traders settled here. They built large and elegant houses on the steep slopes of the main wadi that bisects the town, using the distinctive local yellow limestone. When Amir 'Abdullah chose 'Amman as his capital the fortunes of as-Salt declined. But its charming architecture remains, and the air of a quiet country town; and the houses (as seen by an early traveller) still rise 'one above another like a succession of steps and terraces'.

The heart of as-Salt; the mosque on the hill left of centre is on the site of the ancient citadel

49

Part 2
The North

Jarash

One of the best-preserved provincial Roman towns in the world, Jarash lies about 45 km north of 'Amman, in a fertile valley with a perennial stream. Because of its water, the site has been settled at least since Neolithic times, and Bronze and Iron Age pottery has been found on the original tell. Its early Semitic name was Garshu.

Tradition claims that it was re-founded by Alexander the Great (or perhaps his general Perdiccas) to settle Macedonian veterans; but the Seleucid king Antiochus IV (175-164 BC) is more likely. Renamed Antioch ad Chrysorhoas (Antioch on the Golden River, as the stream was rather grandiosely called), little remains of this Hellenistic era, nor of the brief Hasmonaean occupation, for the new Roman city of Gerasa obliterated most of what preceded it. As a city of the Decapolis, Gerasa entered a long period of prosperity.

In the 1st century AD a new town plan was adopted with a colonnaded main street, the Cardo, at the south end of which is the unusual and lovely Oval Piazza (in fact two unequal parabolas joined by a straight line). Above it is the larger of the two theatres, with seats for about 3,000 people.

Between them is the temple of Zeus, its Hellenistic version on the lower terrace, and its latest 2nd-century AD remodelling on the hill above. Also in the 2nd century the Cardo

Previous pages: The entire site of Jarash, caught in a burst of sunshine; the residential part of the ancient city lies beneath the town on the left of the picture

Right: Jarash's imposing south theatre

was made wider and grander, with Corinthian capitals crowning its columns – the old Ionic ones were reused in various parts of the city. Two cross-streets were made, the North and South Decumanus. West of the Cardo rose a handsome octagonal *macellum*, or food market; and also, just south of the North Decumanus, a second smaller theatre, or odeon. Two large bath houses were added further east, near the residential areas.

Dominating Jarash still is the great temple of Artemis, built and enlarged (but never completed) between the late 1st and mid-2nd centuries, and dedicated to the city's patron goddess. It is set in a wide and spacious *temenos*, approached from the Cardo through a monumental gate and stairway.

In the Byzantine period many churches were built, mainly reusing Roman building material, but Gerasa's heyday was already past when the Persians invaded in 614. After the Arab conquest of 636 the city was an Umayyad regional centre, important enough to mint coins under Caliph 'Abd al-Malik bin Marwan (685-705), and graced with a fine Friday mosque. But after the 749 earthquake and the removal of the Caliphate to Baghdad, the city faded into ruinous obscurity.

In 1806 a young German scholar, Ulrich Seetzen, identified the ruins as Gerasa, and he was soon followed by an increasing stream of western travellers. In 1878 the Ottomans allowed a group of Circassians to settle here; and their village grew into the modern town on the other side of the valley.

Above: The temple of Artemis dominates Gerasa

Right: The Cardo, with the new excavation of the Umayyad mosque by the crossing with the South Decumanus, and the macellum behind it

Following pages: Seen from the north gate, the Cardo runs the full length of Jarash; the north theatre is on the right, with the temple of Artemis above it

'Ajlun

In the hills north-west of Jarash, overlooking the town of 'Ajlun, stands a handsome fort, Qala'at ar-Rabadh, with fine views over the Jordan Valley. A 13th-century Arab writer told of 'an ancient monastery' here, and William of Tyre mentioned a 'small fortress', captured by the Crusaders in 1139. Some incised crosses, and a recently discovered chapel with a mosaic floor (probably 8th-century), give credence to the tradition of a Christian Arab origin.

But the purpose of the present fort was anti-Crusader, built in 1184-85 by 'Izz ad-Din Usama, one of Saladin's generals. This superb piece of Ayyubid military architecture soon outlived its original purpose – in 1187 the Crusaders' defeat at Hattin in Galilee ended their occupation of the Holy Land.

In 1214-15 the castle was enlarged by 'Izz ad-Din Aybak, for the Ayyubid Sultan al-Malik al-Mu'azzam, to become one of the chain of beacons and pigeon stations relaying messages between Damascus and Cairo and, in 1219, housing supplies for use against the Fifth Crusade. In 1260 it fell to the Mongols, but was restored by the Mamluk Sultan Baybars.

Its later history is sketchy – repaired in the 17th century; visited by J. L. Burckhardt in 1812; damaged in an earthquake in 1837; and repaired by Ibrahim Pasha. It was recently repaired and restored by Jordan's Department of Antiquities.

Right: The 12th-C castle at 'Ajlun, built by the Ayyubids as a defence against the Crusaders

Following pages: The King Talal Dam, Jordan's largest reservoir, with a capacity of 85 million cubic metres

59

Tell Deir 'Alla

At the heart of the market town of Deir 'Alla in the Jordan Valley, *c.* 230m below sea level, stands an imposing archaeological mound. Tell Deir 'Alla (mound of the high monastery), has been identified by some scholars as biblical Succoth, and by others as Penuel, both punished by Gideon for refusing to help pursue the Midianites (Judg. 8:4-17). Excavations since the 1960s, by Dutch and Jordanian teams, show that the tell was almost continuously occupied from *c.* 1700 to 400 BC, Middle Bronze Age to the Hellenistic era, though most remains are from the Iron Age.

A large Late Bronze Age sanctuary with associated workshops, contained a quantity of pottery, much of it not locally made. These foreign objects speak of an extensive trade network between Egypt, Mesopotamia, the Levant and Mycene in which the sanctuary played a significant part. It functioned for about 400 years before being destroyed in an earthquake and fire in the early 12th century BC.

The settlement continued to flourish in the Iron Age, still as an important trading station with cultic significance. Among the most important finds were some inscriptions in an early form of Aramaic. One, in black and red ink dating from the 9th century BC '(unique in being written on a wall), recounts a prophecy of Balaam son of Beor, a character who also appears in the Bible (Num. 22-24) in a rather unfavourable light.

The archaeological mound of Tell Deir 'Alla rises above agricultural fields in the Jordan Valley

Pella/Tabaqat Fahl

Set in a fold of the hills that overlook the Jordan Valley, Pella was perfectly situated, not least because of its perennial springs. Their lack of abundance today is due to the modern pump house, which has blemished one of the loveliest sites in Jordan.

Excavations (by Americans in 1958 and 1967; since 1979 by Australians) are stripping back the complex layers of Pella's story. The main tell, inhabited since Neolithic times, includes Chalcolithic and Early Bronze Age settlements; but by far the most significant early monument is on the south side of the tell — a large Middle Bronze Age temple with massive stone walls, built over an earlier mud brick version. This was again rebuilt, but in smaller form, perhaps after an earthquake. More destruction in the Iron Age, in both the 10th and 9th centuries BC, led to more rebuilding, each smaller than the one before.

The first literary reference to the site is also Middle Bronze Age, in the 19th century BC, when it is referred to in Egyptian texts as Pihilum, or Pehel. It was an active trade centre, which had links with Syria and Cyprus as well as with Egypt, for whom it supplied wood for making chariot spokes.

On the division of Alexander's Empire its name was changed to Pella — either to honour Alexander's birthplace, or as a Hellenisation of Pehel, or both. Its Arabic name too, Tabaqat

Pella, overlooking the Jordan Valley; Tell al-Husn is on the left, the main tell is outlined by the winding road on the right, with a church and theatre between them; the east church is in a patch of sunlight bottom right

65

Fahl, comes from this ancient name, for 'f' in Arabic derives from Aramaic 'p'.

Pella changed hands recurrently between the Ptolemies and Seleucids, and in 83 BC was sacked by Alexander Jannaeus. After liberation by Pompey in 63 BC, its fortunes improved as a city of the Decapolis. Its only surviving Roman monuments are the scant remains of a small theatre, a bath house and a nymphaeum, and a fine wall of a temple of Serapis on the south side of the main church.

In AD 67 Pella provided a refuge for some Christians fleeing the Roman destruction of Jerusalem. Later it became an episcopal see, and its bishops attended the Ecumenical Councils of the church. Prosperity continued in the Byzantine period, when the settlement expanded and several churches were built.

In 635 the first victory of the new Islamic army over the Byzantines occurred near Pella, followed a year later by another victory near the Yarmouk river further north. Pella was a thriving Umayyad town for just over 100 years, with an attractive residential area on the tell. Some fine Umayyad pottery has been found here, made in the Jarash kilns. But the city was virtually destroyed in the massive earthquake of 749 – in one of the houses excavators found the entwined skeletons of a man and woman, who clung together in fear when the earthquake struck. The woman was wearing a gown of Chinese silk.

The site continued to be occupied in the Abbasid and Mamluk periods, but it was now a smaller and more rural community. A mud-brick village still stood on the tell until 1967-68, when the villagers moved further down the hill to avoid Israeli air raids.

Above: Excavations at the site of a Middle Bronze Age temple; a Mamluk mosque stands behind it

Right: Roman and Byzantine monuments in Pella — the church, on top of a temple of Serapis, stands beside the remains of a small theatre

Gadara/Umm Qays

Little is known of the earliest history of Gadara, a hilltop site in the north-west corner of Jordan with grand views over Lake Tiberias, the Yarmouk river and the Golan Heights. It is associated with the story of Jesus casting out demons and sending them into a herd of pigs which rushed down a steep slope and drowned in the lake (Matt. 8:28-34). The exact location of the miracle is unknown, but it could hardly have been Gadara itself as it is too far from the lake.

In the Hellenistic era Gadara changed hands like most of Jordan between the Ptolemies and the Seleucids – parts of the city wall and the base of a temple date to this time. It was taken by Alexander Jannaeus in 83 BC, and some Nabataean finds indicate that they too were here briefly. Liberated from Hasmonaean rule by Pompey in 63 BC, its full glory came in the Roman period as one of the Decapolis cities.

Gadara was noted for its rich intellectual life and as the birthplace of several famous philosophers and poets of the ancient world, in particular the Cynic philosopher Menippus who lived in the 3rd century BC, and Meleager and Philodemos in the 1st century BC. The Gadarenes also revelled in the famous hot springs in the valley below, after which, wrote Strabo, they returned to 'the cooler heights of the city, solacing their leisure with plays performed in the theatres'.

Previous pages: A hill-top olive orchard near Jarash
Right: The 5-aisled basilica, built in the 4th C for pilgrims visiting the site of one of Christ's miracles

Of the two theatres at Gadara (a third was in the valley), the smaller western one is the better preserved, its black basalt seats accommodating an audience of 3,000. Beside it are the remains of a 7th-century basilica and a 6th-century octagonal church. On either side of the long colonnaded street excavations since 1974 have revealed public and private bath complexes, a nymphaeum, a sanctuary, octagonal and semi-circular buildings, a round tower (one of two that formed a huge city gate), an underground mausoleum and, above it, a large 4th-century church with five aisles. Further west are another two monumental gates and the outline of a hippodrome.

Prosperity continued throughout the Byzantine era when Gadara was the seat of a bishop. Its association with one of Jesus' miracles gave it high status as a place of pilgrimage, and the five-aisled basilica may well have been built to accommodate pilgrims. Though continuing to flourish after the Islamic conquest of 636, decline set in after the overthrow in 750 of the Umayyads by the Abbasids, who moved the centre of the Caliphate east to Baghdad.

An abandoned field of ruins when the first western travellers visited it in the 19th century, Gadara's ancient monuments were ransacked for building stone at the end of that century, and a village of great charm grew up amongst the ruins. When archaeological work began in 1974, the villagers were moved into new housing nearby, and some of their handsome Arab houses are being restored alongside the excavation of the classical site.

Previous pages: Gadara overlooks Lake Tiberias and the southern Golan Heights; the hollow of the north theatre is right of the Ottoman village, with the scant remains of a Hellenistic temple further to the right; the colonnaded street runs due west

Top left: One of the pentagonal towers in the Hellenistic city wall

Top right: An exedra beside the Cardo whose original function is unclear; it was later used as a church

Below: An octagonal building, probably a market, very similar to that at Jarash

Right: The black basalt west theatre, with the basilica terrace and courtyard beyond it, and part of the Ottoman village to its right

Umm al-Jimal

The black basalt city of Umm al-Jimal (its name means 'mother of camels') lies like a dark encrustation on the flat plains of north Jordan. So many buildings still stand to two or three storeys that it looks as if it was abandoned within living memory – in fact it was about 1,200 years ago.

The Nabataeans established a base here in the 1st century AD as a staging post on the trade route between Damascus and the south. With no springs or wells, the entire water supply had to be gathered in hundreds of cisterns during the rainy season.

After the 106 AD Roman annexation of the Nabataean kingdom, Umm al-Jimal was enlarged, becoming an important military base, with encircling walls, a new reservoir, and a hydraulic system to supply this and its other cisterns and reservoirs. A vast (now ruinous) fort was also constructed, to be replaced by a considerably smaller barracks in the early 5th century, when the military role of the city had declined.

In the Byzantine era more houses were built, 14 churches and a cathedral; and growth continued under the Umayyads, still with its Christian community. But after the 749 earthquake and the Abbasid removal to Baghdad it was never rebuilt. It remained abandoned until the early 20th century, when some Druze from nearby Jabal al-'Arab took up brief residence here. The modern village near the ruins dates from 1950.

The black basalt city of Umm al-Jimal, with the Byzantine barracks on the right

76

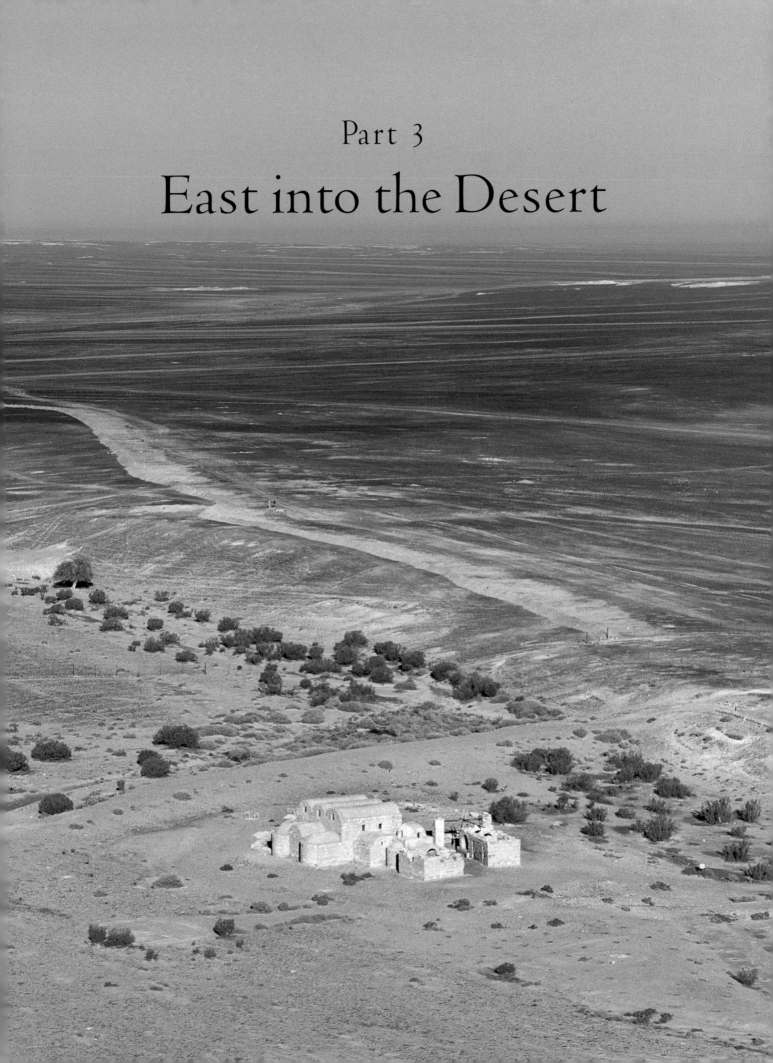

Part 3
East into the Desert

Qasr at-Tuba

In 1896 Alois Musil, a Czech explorer and Arabist, was told by the bedouin of Madaba of some old palaces in the desert, adorned with columns, paintings and inscriptions. On his return two years later, he found Qasr at-Tuba, the largest and most remote of a group of desert residences built in the early 8th century under the auspices of the Umayyad caliphs. Called *qasr* (palace) in Arabic and castle in English, they are in fact neither. All are enchanting examples of early Islamic architecture, individual in style and materials; and all had an agricultural base.

The Umayyad caliphs and their governors doubtless relished an escape from Damascus to the unconfining desert, where they could hawk and hunt and race their Arab horses. But a more serious purpose underlay these buildings – they provided meeting places for contacts with the bedouin tribes of the desert, on whose support they depended.

Qasr at-Tuba, built in the time of Caliph al-Walid II (743-44), consists of two equal enclosures making a double square. Only the north corner was completed but the outline of the whole complex is clear from the air. The walls are of three courses of stone with baked mud brick above, including the barrel-vaulted roofs. Stone was also used to frame the door arches. Musil found some fine stone carvings but these have disappeared, apart from one lintel now in the 'Amman Archaeological Museum.

Previous pages: Qusayr 'Amra and the wild pistachio trees of Wadi Butm in the desert east of 'Amman

Qasr at-Tuba, the most remote of Jordan's Umayyad desert residences, was never completed

Azraq oasis

Azraq, whose name means 'blue', lies 80km east of 'Amman in a vast shallow basin surrounding an oasis. Here three deserts meet – black basalt in north and east Jordan, flint and limestone in the centre, and the sand of Wadi Sirhan, running into Saudi Arabia.

Many millions of years ago most of Jordan was under the sea; one million years ago the waters had receded, leaving a huge lake in the Azraq basin, which reduced further to create fertile plains and extensive marshes teeming with animals and birds. Today it is desert, with shrinking swamps and pools at its heart, and dying palm trees. This is a recent escalation, as water has been pumped in vast quantities to meet the ever increasing needs of a fast-growing population in a land with exiguous water resources.

Until recently Azraq was rich in migrating birds, en route between Europe and Africa – as the swamps diminished, so did the birds. However, Jordan's Royal Society for the Conservation of Nature (RSCN) has created a wetlands reserve at Azraq Shishan (named after its 19th-century Chechen settlers), in a small area of the original marshes. A fraction of Azraq's spring water is being diverted into pools beside a large Umayyad reservoir – and some birds are returning.

The RSCN also established the nearby Shaumari Reserve in 1967, the first wildlife reserve in Jordan; its greatest success is the re-introduction of the Arabian oryx into its natural habitat.

Part of the Azraq Wetlands Reserve, restored by the Royal Society for the Conservation of Nature, where many varieties of birds can still be seen

A group of Arabian oryx (Oryx leucoryx) in the Shaumari Wildlife Reserve

Azraq castle

Azraq's abundant water made it an obvious stopping place on the Wadi Sirhan trade route, and a magnet for desert bedouins. It also attracted the Romans who, under Septimius Severus (AD 193-211), established here an eastern military outpost of the Province of Arabia. If that was the first phase of the castle at the centre of Azraq Druze, there is little to show for it, for it went through several later incarnations.

A stone-carved dedication to the co-Emperors Diocletian and Maximian, dated to c. AD 300, may mark the beginning of the black basalt fort, whose huge stone doors still turn on their original hinges. Diocletian also built a road here, the Strata Diocletiana, linking Azraq to Damascus and Palmyra.

Azraq remained a military post throughout the Byzantine period, and in the 7th and 8th centuries the Umayyads came here to hunt. The fort may have been neglected after the Abbasids moved to Baghdad – according to an Arabic inscription over the main gate, the Ayyubid governor 'Izz ad-Din Aybak rebuilt it in the early 13th century. The Ottomans garrisoned it after their conquest in 1516.

Azraq's most recent military use was in World War I, when T. E. Lawrence stayed in the fort in the winter of 1917-18, before the final assault on Damascus. A few years later some Syrian Druze moved to this northern part of Azraq, and here they remain.

The black basalt fort at Azraq; most of what we see today is 13th-C Ayyubid work, but its origins are Roman

Qusayr 'Amra

Two days after finding Qasr at-Tuba, Alois Musil saw Qusayr (little palace) 'Amra, a harmonious stone building in Wadi Butm, named after the wild pistachios (*butm*) growing here. Inside are vivid frescos, some still in fair condition despite centuries of neglect, bedouin fires and graffiti.

The date is unclear – after 711 and maybe as late as Caliph al-Walid II. Perhaps originally part of a larger complex, what we see today are an audience hall of three parallel barrel-vaults, with an alcove and two small rooms off it; and a bath house of three rooms, including a domed *calidarium* with under-floor hypocaust heating. Outside is a well-house and a structure for raising water.

The frescos are exceptional, not only for their joyous naturalism, but for their very existence. The first edict against human images was by Caliph Yazid II (720-24) when these frescos, with their free depictions of human life, may already have been painted – hunting scenes; personifications of History, Philosophy and Poetry; musicians; dancers; women and children bathing in varying states of déshabillé; and six contemporary rulers paying homage: the Byzantine and Sassanian Emperors, the Visigoth King of Spain, the Negus of Abyssinia, and possibly the King of India and the Emperor of China. Most remarkable is the fresco in the little dome of the *calidarium* – the earliest known representation of the night sky in the round.

Qusayr 'Amra, with the three barrel vaults of the audience hall and the dome of the bath house; the well is in front

87

Qasr al-Kharanah

This is one of only two of Jordan's desert castles that seem to be built for defence. But here this may be more apparent than real — the 'arrow-slits' are too high and small and must have been for air and light. Nor was it a caravanserai as it is not on a trade route. Most likely it was a place where the Umayyad rulers could meet with bedouin of the desert, to negotiate their support.

The castle is built of undressed stones, with smaller stones laid in rows between them; it was originally plastered all over. Its uncompromising squareness is broken by a round tower at each corner and a semi-circular one in the middle of each wall, except on the south side where the sole entrance occupies the centre.

The building consists of two storeys around an open courtyard. The stables are to left and right just inside the gate, while accommodation for human beings is around the three other sides of the courtyard and on the upper floors. In one of the upper rooms a painted Kufic inscription over a door bears the date 92 AH (AD 710-11), in the reign of Walid I, but it is unclear if this refers to the original construction or a later rebuilding.

A feature of Qasr al-Kharanah is the use of arches and vaults in every room, many with semi-domes and squinches; arches also spring from groups of three small engaged columns. All the rooms were plastered and carved with decorative patterns.

The fortress-like Qasr al-Kharanah; the trunk road to Iraq, electricity pylons and a telecommunications relay station have encroached on its desert isolation

Qasr al-Hallabat

This considerable complex includes the *qasr* itself, a mosque, a large reservoir, cisterns, an agricultural enclosure and a bath house. New excavations at the *qasr* and the mosque have led to a reassessment of the history of the site.

While pottery and inscriptions suggest a Nabataean phase, the present *qasr* probably began as a small 2nd-century Roman fort, one of many defending the Arabian frontier, the *limes arabicus*. It was built of local limestone and guarded the Via Nova Traiana. Later it was rebuilt on a plan four times the original size, with a square tower at each corner.

This second fort was destroyed in the 6th century, perhaps in the 551 earthquake, and was again rebuilt, probably by the Christian Ghassanid tribe. While the exterior still kept the appearance of a fort, the interior became a residence with an audience hall, decorated with marble and mosaics. Many black basalt stones were brought in from elsewhere for this rebuilding. Some bear sections of a long Greek inscription, an edict of Emperor Anastasius I (491-518), defining his reorganisation of the Province of Arabia; but the stones were used with no regard for the inscriptions, which were plastered over.

The *qasr*'s greatest glory came in the 8th century, when the Umayyads transformed it into a palatial residence, lavishly adorned with carved stucco, frescos and vivid mosaic floors. A handsome mosque was built beside it. And 2km away are the remains of a bath house (Hammam as-Sarah), very similar in style to that of Qusayr 'Amra.

Qasr al-Hallabat (right), originally built as a Roman fort and rebuilt several times up to the 8th C; and (above), Hammam as-Sarah, the bath house associated with it

Qasr al-Mushatta

T he most richly decorated of the Umayyad palaces in Jordan was Qasr al-Mushatta, near Queen 'Alia International Airport just south of 'Amman. Little remains of the delicate and vivid stone carvings that once adorned the façade – in 1903 the Ottoman Sultan Abdul Hamid II gave them to Kaiser Wilhelm II. They are now in Berlin.

Qasr al-Mushatta is a large square walled enclosure with round towers at the corners and five semi-circular ones at regular intervals on each side except the south, whose centre is occupied by the gateway. It was on either side of this gate that the magnificent 5-metre high carvings were originally situated in a band of upright and inverted triangles. Those on the left of the gate were adorned with images showing the peaceful coexistence of animals and mythological creatures; those on the right had vine and flower motifs with no animal or human figures, probably because of the mosque immediately behind.

A complex of buildings just inside the gate led into a spacious central court, with the royal audience hall and residence at the far end, probably built for Caliph Walid II. The audience hall is basilical as you enter from the court, with a trefoil apse which may have been covered by a wooden dome. On either side of it the buildings were covered with barrel vaults of baked mud bricks, some of which remain. Like Qasr at-Tuba, the palace was never completed.

The most richly decorated of the Umayyad residences was Qasr al-Mushatta, but the carvings were taken to the Pergamon Museum in Berlin in 1903

Part 4
Central Jordan

Umm ar-Rasas

Umm ar-Rasas lies in open rolling countryside just east of Dhiban. First mentioned in the Bible as Mephaath (Josh. 13:18), it was later one of the many Moabite towns that Jeremiah prophesied against (Jer. 48:21). In Roman times it was Castron Mefaath, or Mefa'a, and indeed the main ruins are a Roman fort the size of a small town (158 x 139m), where a Roman garrison was based. But time and earthquakes have reduced it to a chaos of fallen stones, with some arches rising above the rubble.

Previous pages: The Roman reservoir near Qasr Bshir, still used for watering local flocks

Right: Umm ar-Rasas, a large Roman castellum with many Byzantine- and Umayyad-period churches

Below: A 6th-C hermit's tower at Umm ar-Rasas, with a church on its left and a 3-storey building on the right

Four churches have been identified inside the walls, two of which have been excavated, both 6th century. Outside the northern walls the excavation of several more churches has revealed some magnificent mosaic floors of the late-6th to 8th centuries. Most spectacular is that in St Stephen's Church (laid in 719; the apse in 756), which includes representations of cities in Palestine, Jordan and Egypt – with no false modesty, 'Kastron Mefaa' and Jerusalem occupy the two positions of honour in the design. Clearly Christian life continued uninterrupted after the 636 Islamic conquest, with large churches being built and lavishly adorned.

Two kilometres north of the fort stands a tall tower, with a cross carved on three sides and a single chamber at the top. It is thought to have been a stylite's pillar of the 6th century. Near it are a small church, a three-storey building and rock-cut cisterns.

Dhiban

All that is now visible of ancient Dibon is a partly excavated tell beside the present-day village of Dhiban, just north of the spectacular Wadi al-Mujib gorge, biblical Arnon (see photo on pp. 102-103). Though it had an Early Bronze Age settlement, the period about which most is known is the Iron Age, especially the 9th century BC, when it was the capital of Mesha, king of Moab.

Inscribed on the Mesha stele (in an early script very close to Hebrew) is the king's claim that he liberated and rebuilt towns in Moab, previously captured by Israel. At Dibon he built a high place for his god, Chemosh, and repaired 'the parkland walls... the walls of the acropolis; and... its gates,... towers and... the king's residence'. He also restored the town's water supply and made every household have its own cistern.

Parts of the massive 9th-century defences were revealed in excavations in the 1950s to 60s; so too was a Nabataean temple, a tower which may have been part of the Roman fortifications, and a Byzantine church.

When the black basalt Mesha stele was found here in 1868, the news caused a flurry of bidding between the Prussian and French Consuls. Convinced the stone held treasure, the local bedouin smashed it to pieces. But a Frenchman, Charles Clermont-Ganneau, had made a squeeze of it and, when he collected the pieces, the stele could be reconstructed. It can be seen in the Louvre in Paris

The tell of Iron Age Dibon, capital of King Mesha of Moab in the 9th C BC

Al-Lahun

D**ramatically** located on the very edge of the northern cliff of Wadi al-Mujib, the site of Lahun was recurrently reoccupied from earliest times up to the present. Rather than take over the ruins of their predecessors, each new wave of settlers preferred to start again on untouched ground.

The Early Bronze Age settlement here, home to an agricultural community from the late 4th millennium BC, was later fortified with huge walls, as were other towns at this period. Clearly the region had become less stable and the villagers felt an increased need to defend themselves against attack. One of their crops was olives, for stone presses for making olive oil have been found here.

Next was an Early Iron Age village with some unusual pillared houses, completely surrounded by a double wall (with rooms in the intervening space). Later a fort was built at the south end, in a commanding position on the rim of Wadi al-Mujib. In the 9th century BC it might have been a storehouse for King Mesha of Moab's nearby garrison. The site was abandoned not long after.

The next wave of occupation – again in a new location – came several centuries later when the area was part of the Nabataean kingdom. The main monument from this period is a small temple. In the same area there are also some Roman, Mamluk and Ottoman remains.

Al-Lahun, a multi-period site beside Wadi al-Mujib – the Iron Age fort is on the edge of the wadi on the right

Following pages: The great gorge of Wadi al-Mujib, which runs west into the Dead Sea

Qasr Bshir

The Latin inscription above the main gate of this unusually well preserved Roman fort records that it was built in AD 293-305 by Aurelius Asclepiades, then governor of the province of Arabia, and dedicated to the co-Emperors Diocletian and Maximian, 'our best and greatest rulers', and to their two Caesars. It was one of a string of forts, within a day's march of each other, built at a time of increased insecurity in the Roman Province of Arabia. There were also watchtowers between the forts, so that signals could be sent rapidly from one to another should troops be needed.

Qasr Bshir is almost square in shape, with the longest side, which has the main entrance in the middle, on the south-west. The central courtyard was surrounded by rooms on two levels, the lower ones with mangers built into the walls – perhaps an indication that the fort was a base for a cavalry unit. The upper rooms were probably occupied by soldiers. At each of the four corners stands a square tower, three storeys high, in one corner of which a square spiral stairway leads to the upper floors.

The fort was well supplied with water – three cisterns have been found outside the walls, and there are two cut into the ground in the central courtyard. Also, about 500m to the south-west is a large reservoir, also Roman in date. It is still in use, providing local farmers with water for their flocks.

The well-preserved Qasr Bshir, one of a string of forts the Romans built to defend their Province of Arabia

Karak

This splendid Crusader fortress – Crak des Moabites, or Le Pierre du Désert to the Crusaders – soars above the wadis and hills like a great ship riding waves of rock. It is strategically situated in the midst of rich agricultural land, on the ancient crossroads between the north-south trade route of the King's Highway, and the east-west route that climbs Wadi Karak from the Dead Sea and runs to the edge of the eastern desert.

Karak's origins go back at least to the Late Bronze Age. In the Iron Age, as Kir-haraseth, it was a major town of Moab under King Mesha (c. 853-830 BC). Later it also figured in Isaiah's prophecies, in which he rather oddly mixed messages of doom with mention of what may have been a local delicacy, now unknown – 'Let everyone wail for Moab. Mourn, utterly stricken, for the raisin-cakes of Kir-hareseth' (Is. 16:7).

Carvings, column drums and inscriptions indicate that this was a significant town in Nabataean, Roman and Byzantine times – it minted its own coins in the 3rd century, and appears prominently in the Madaba mosaic map as Characmoba. But these earlier towns were obliterated by the new Crusader castle.

The Crusader province east of the Jordan rift, Oultrejourdain, was at first based at Montréal (Shobak). But in 1142 the lord of the province, Payan le Bouteiller, judging Karak's position more strategic, began work on this new castle. It was completed by the de Milly family, lords of the province after 1161, who lived here in a more grandiose style than that of any western king.

In 1177 Etiennette de Milly, heiress of Oultrejourdain, took as her third husband Renaud de Châtillon, one of the most ruthless and duplicitous of all the Crusaders. After Renaud's repeated attacks on Muslim pilgrimage caravans and ships in 1181 and 1182, in defiance of a truce, the Ayyubid leader Saladin vowed revenge. His siege of Karak in 1183 coincided with the marriage of Etiennette's son, Humfried von Toron, to Princess Isabella of Jerusalem. Etiennette diplomatically sent wedding food to Saladin, who then asked which tower housed the bridal pair and ordered his siege engines to cease bombarding it. In the end he had to raise the siege, as he did again the next year.

After the defeat of the Crusaders at the battle of Hattin in 1187, such was Saladin's fury with Renaud (who had continued his brutal raids on pilgrims) that he personally beheaded him. In 1188, after a siege of over a year, Karak finally surrendered to Saladin's army – the alternative was starvation.

Karak remained in Ayyubid hands until the Mamluk Sultan Baybars took it in 1264. He and his heirs rebuilt much of the castle, which in 1355 impressed the Arab traveller Ibn Battuta – he said it was called 'the Castle of the Raven'. In Ottoman times Karak was ruled by local families. It became a British administrative centre after World War I until the Emirate of Transjordan was founded in 1921. It remains the centre of a large district.

Karak's 12th-C Crusader castle on its pinnacle of rock, as it was in 1985. It was never taken by storm but had to be starved into surrender

The Dead Sea

J ordan's western border runs below sea level
for most of its 360km length, following
the line of the Jordan rift. At its heart is
the Dead Sea, over 400m below sea level – the
lowest place on earth. It is part of the Great
Rift Valley, which runs from southern Turkey
through Syria, Jordan and the Red Sea, west
into East Africa and south to Mozambique.

The cataclysms that created the rift began
some 30 million years ago and recurred until
c. 15,000 years ago, forming mountains which
on the east rise to around 1,500m above the
Dead Sea. Until 100,000 years ago the rift
was an extension of the Red Sea; then the waters
receded, forming the saline Lake Lisan, 200m
higher than today's Dead Sea. By *c.* 10,000 BC
this had shrunk further, leaving the Dead Sea
and Lake Tiberias, linked by the Jordan Valley.

Tiberias became a freshwater lake, but the
Dead Sea, with no outlet, remained saline. As
the sources of the Jordan river are diverted by
Israel and Jordan taps its streams for its own
needs, the Dead Sea's level has fallen sharply
in the past 50 years – it is still falling by about
one metre a year; and the rift is still moving.

Bitumen was harvested annually from the
Dead Sea by the Nabataeans, and profitably
sold to the Egyptians for their embalming
process; now it rarely appears. Today's major
product is potash; also table salt and cosmetic
and therapeutic preparations.

*Previous pages: The western end of Wadi Karak, with
the Dead Sea in the distance*

*The Dead Sea at its southern end, with evaporation
pools for extracting minerals*

Lot's church, Safi

In the hills east of Ghor as-Safi (ancient Zoar) a cave was found in 1991 with Early and Middle Bronze Age pottery inside. Speculation linked the finds with Abraham's nephew Lot who, according to the Bible, moved to a cave in the hills above Zoar after the destruction of Sodom and Gomorrah.

In the Bible (Gen. 19:30-38), Lot's two daughters, afraid of being the last people left on earth, plied their father with wine and slept with him in turn. The elder daughter bore a son named Moab, ancestor of the Moabites, while the younger daughter's son, Ben-ammi, was the father of the Ammonites. The story smacks of the kind of propaganda any tribe might put out to discredit its enemies – tales told by the Moabites and Ammonites against the Israelites do not survive.

The area has long been associated with Lot – the 6th-century Madaba map shows a church of St Lot in just this location. And excavations here in the 1990s revealed a 7th-century Byzantine church with a dedication to 'St Lot', and with access to the cave through the north apse. Its floors were covered with six mosaic pavements, one dated 572, another April 605, a third May 691. The size of the church, its associated hostel, and inscriptions invoking the name of Lot, all point to this being a place of pilgrimage. It continued to be so for more than a century after the Islamic conquest.

Previous pages: Ghor as-Safi, where the fresh waters of Wadi Hasa run into the southern end of the Dead Sea

The Church of St Lot in the hills above Ghor as-Safi

Part 5
Petra and the Nabataean Kingdom

Petra

Ancient Petra lies in the dramatic barrier of multicoloured sandstone mountains that run parallel with Wadi 'Araba. Formed by the primeval cataclysms that grooved the Jordan rift, the mountains were then sculpted by millions of years of wind, rain and earthquakes into the landscape of a dream.

Scattered among these exuberant forms of nature are some of the most prodigious works of man, carved into sheer rock faces some 2,000 years ago by the Nabataeans, originally an itinerant tribe from the Arabian peninsula. No one knows when they first started coming to Petra; it may have been as early as the 6th century BC, as traders moving along the route by which their most valuable trade goods — frankincense and myrrh — were carried from south-west Arabia, where they grew, to Gaza, for export to Europe.

There is no evidence of the Nabataeans in Petra until 312 BC, by which time they had already acquired vast wealth through trade. It was a time when Alexander the Great's generals were fighting for his empire and one of them, Antigonus the One-Eyed, attacked when the Nabataean men were at a national gathering, leaving women, children, old people and treasure on top of a high rock, either in Petra itself or nearby. Having massacred many of them, the Greeks made off with a huge quantity of silver and incense — only to be caught sleeping by the pursuing Nabataeans and slaughtered.

Previous pages: The sanctuary of Moses' brother Aaron on Jabal Haroun, just south-west of Petra

Right: Sandstone mountains in wild shapes and colours surround the Nabataean capital

Although they had kings at least from 168 BC, it was only in the early 1st century BC that the Nabataeans began to settle, and to transform their occasional base at Petra into a magnificent capital. Their technology was simple: picks and chisels levelled mountain tops to form high places for worship of the gods; they cut stairways to reach them; grooved channels to bring water from miles around; and built fine temples, palaces, market places and houses. And they carved hauntingly beautiful architectural façades in the rock in honour of their dead.

To defend their territory, or to expand it, the Nabataeans fought recurrent wars with Judah and Syria. Aretas II (*c.* 100-96 BC), his son Obodas I (96-86 BC) and grandson Aretas III (86-62 BC) all extended their land, largely at Syria's expense as the Seleucid state fell apart. But when Pompey annexed Syria in 64 BC, the Nabataeans had to deal with Rome's Province of Syria in the north and their client state of Judaea in the west.

The Nabataeans remained independent by careful diplomacy with Rome, exercised by kings blessed with longevity. Greatest of all was Aretas IV (9 BC-AD 40), who initiated many of Petra's finest monuments. The last two Nabataean kings, Malichus II (AD 40-70) and Rabbel II (AD 70-106), spent more time in Bostra (in today's Syria), which became an alternative capital. When Rabbel died in 106, the Roman legate of Syria annexed his kingdom in the name of the Emperor Trajan and incorporated it as the major part of the new Roman Province of Arabia.

From the Treasury to the theatre

At the end of the long twilight of the Siq — the cleft in the rock that was and is the most famous entrance to the city — we emerge in front of the glowing façade of the Treasury (al-Khazneh), elaborately carved with floral motifs and Nabataean and Greek gods and mythological figures — Castor and Pollux, with horses, guiding the souls of the dead; axe-wielding Amazons; winged Victories; eagles and a Medusa head. All are funerary symbols. Presiding over them is al-'Uzza, the main goddess of Petra, here linked with the Greek goddesses Aphrodite and Tyche, and also Isis, the Egyptian goddess, who ruled the underworld and spirits of the dead.

With its wealth of funerary symbolism, the Treasury was clearly connected with the Nabataean cult of the dead, but its date and function are unclear. Some scholars think it may have been commissioned by Aretas IV — a theory reinforced by the discovery in 2003 of some earlier tombs carved into the rock at the foot of the Treasury, containing pottery shards from the second half of the 1st century BC.

Beyond the Treasury, the Outer Siq leads to the 5,000-seat theatre, carved right in the middle of a major cemetery area with no apparent sense of incongruity. Though Roman in design, it is Nabataean in the style of its execution, and may have been carved from the rock in the time of Aretas IV. But there are no clues as to what was performed here. Were there Greek classics? Works of home-grown Nabataean dramatists? Comedy, tragedy, or religious presentations? We do not know.

Petra's theatre was cut out of the rock in the middle of the necropolis in the 1st C AD

Left: The Outer Siq leads from the Treasury to the theatre, with the Petra basin visible beyond

Tombs and temples

Tombs carved in al-Khubtha mountain are designated 'royal' from their magnificence – who but Nabataean kings, it is supposed, would have such grand tombs? But which king was buried in which tomb is unknown.

First on the left, the vast Palace Tomb is named from its likeness to a Roman palace. Next is the eroded Corinthian tomb, a less aesthetic copy of the Treasury, perhaps made for Malichus II. To its right are some smaller tombs that hardly warrant being called 'royal'; but one has vivid rock strata, like moiré silk – hence its name: the Silk tomb.

The tall Urn tomb, named after the small urn at the top, is called by the bedouin *al-mahkamah* (court of justice), and the vaults supporting the terrace *as-sijn* (prison) – perhaps myth, or reflecting a later use. Dated to the mid-1st century AD, it could have been made for Malichus II, or for his father, Aretas IV, some 30 years earlier. In 446 it was converted into a church.

Ringed around with its fine tomb façades, Petra may seem like a grand cemetery – but it was primarily a place for the living, and for worship. The 1st-century BC building called Qasr al-Bint was probably the city's main temple. Across the wadi another temple is named after carvings found in it – the Temple of the Winged Lions. And the newly excavated 'Great Temple' may not have been a temple at all – perhaps a royal or civic meeting hall. Originally built in the 1st century BC, it was later transformed by having a 600-seat theatre built inside it.

Petra's Royal tombs, carved into the base of Jabal al-Khubtha – from left to right: the Palace tomb, the Corinthian tomb, 3 smaller tombs (Silk tomb in the middle) and the Urn tomb

Gods and high places

The Nabataeans' main gods were those of ancient Arabia – Dushara, their great god; al-Kutba (trade and writing); Shay' al-Qaum (guardian of caravans); and three goddesses: al-'Uzza, 'Allat and Manat, of whom al-'Uzza was supreme in Petra. The Nabataeans adopted the Edomite Qos and Syrian Hadad, both storm gods; and the Syrian goddess Atargatis, who oversaw fertility, vegetation and rain. They also identified their gods with those of Egypt, Greece and Rome. One deity, known from inscriptions as 'Zeus Obodas' or 'Obodas the god', may have been King Obodas I, deified after his death in 85 BC.

The main early place of worship of the Nabataeans – the High Place of Sacrifice – overlooks Petra from the crest of a mountain, levelled for the purpose, with a rectangular court and altars cut into the rock. No one knows who was worshipped here, but it was probably Dushara and al-'Uzza.

On another crest stands the Monastery (ad-Deir), which may be associated with Obodas I. Its current name comes from a later Christian use but it was originally a hall for memorial feasts. An inscription by the path that leads up to the Monastery could indicate who was honoured here for it mentions the sacred association of 'Obodas the god'. His cult still flourished over a century after he died, for the Deir dates to the 1st century AD.

This vast and harmonious façade was modelled on the Treasury, but with no figurative carving – perhaps its creators felt that the plainer form was more beautiful, or more in keeping with the Nabataean ethos.

On the crest of Jabal Madhbah (centre right) the rectangular High Place of Sacrifice is carved into the rock; below left are two obelisks, perhaps representing deities

Right: The vast façade of the Monastery, dwarfed by the surrounding mountains

Al-Beidha

A short distance north of Petra lies an area of pale honey coloured rock – al-Beidha in Arabic, 'the white one'. Here in the 1st century AD the Nabataeans established a commercial suburb, a place for trading caravans to stop en route between south Arabia and the Mediterranean.

Al-Beidha's fertile land had been exploited for many millennia before the Nabataeans. A Neolithic group settled here around 7000 BC, hunting animals with flint weapons and gathering wild plants to eat. They also grew wheat and barley and kept goats and sheep. International trade is clear from Anatolian obsidian found here, turquoise from Sinai and pumice and shells from the Red Sea and the Mediterranean, doubtless exchanged for local red haematite, red and yellow ochres, green malachite, and shiny, translucent mica.

Eight building levels have been excavated, from groups of circular rooms with shared walls to rectangular houses. Though hearths were outside in courtyards, fires still occurred, followed by rebuilding. It is one of the best preserved of Neolithic settlements, for it was never built on again after its abandonment some 500 years after it was settled. The only damage came 6,000 years later, when the Nabataeans terraced these fields for farming.

Today al-Beidha is part of the territory of the Amareen bedouin, who farm the land and use the Nabataeans' rock-cut cisterns.

The Neolithic village at al-Beidha

Following pages: Amareen bedouin with black goat-hair tents at Beidha; right, a woman weaves tent cloth

Khirbet at-Tannur

This spectacularly sited Nabataean temple and pilgrimage centre lies some 100km north of Petra, crowning a conical hill that rises in the heart of Wadi al-Hasa. No village is associated with the site, which was excavated by an American team in 1936-37.

The first small Nabataean altar, almost cubic in shape, was built here in the late 1st century BC on what may have been an Edomite high place. Among its ruins the excavators found charred remains of the wheat and small animals that pilgrims had sacrificed to their gods 2,000 years before.

About 100 years later, the sanctuary was expanded to occupy the entire mountain top. A paved sacred precinct, colonnaded on two sides and with four halls (*triclinia*) for ritual feasts, surrounded the larger altar that now enclosed the earlier one. Inside were enthroned statues of the deities to whom the temple was dedicated: the Edomite Qos and Syrian Atargatis. A more spectacular carving of Atargatis crowned the entrance, leaves growing on her face and neck and with an eagle above her head, an attribute of Qos. This and other carvings suggest a cycle of worship based on the agricultural calendar.

In the 2nd century the temple was again expanded, and more statues were added, in particular of Atargatis, some with sheaves of grain or a dolphin on her head. The site continued to function as a pilgrimage centre until the late 3rd or mid-4th century AD.

The conical hill of Jabal at-Tannur in Wadi Hasa, on whose summit the Nabataeans created a sanctuary and pilgrimage centre

Khirbet adh-Dharih

Early in the 1st century AD a Nabataean settlement was built on an abandoned Edomite site not far from Khirbet at-Tannur. It was well situated, being beside the King's Highway and near three abundant springs. Judging by the three olive presses that were found here, the inhabitants were active farmers and in time their little settlement expanded into a village.

At the beginning of the 2nd century AD — either late in the reign of Rabbel II or early in the Roman period — the small temple here was replaced by one that was larger and more lavishly decorated. Relief carvings of gods and mythological figures, such as Hermes, Pan, Castor and Pollux and others, all representing signs of the zodiac, formed a spectacular frieze on the temple's main façade. The dominance of the zodiac suggests that the Nabataeans' main agricultural festivals were celebrated here.

The size of the temple and its precinct in relation to the small village, and the presence near the temple of a hostel building, indicate that this site, like nearby Khirbet at-Tannur, was a pilgrimage centre. The precinct was not completed until around AD 150, well into the Roman period, and the life of the sanctuary and village seem to have continued without interruption until they were destroyed in the 363 earthquake and abandoned.

The sanctuary (but not the village) was reoccupied in the 6th century and the temple was reoriented and converted into a church; it continued in use until the early Abbasid period when it was again abandoned.

Above: The temple at the far end of pilgrimage site was converted into a church in the 6th C

Left: The Nabataean village (foreground) at Khirbet adh-Dharih, with its temple and pilgrimage centre on the edge of the wadi

133

Al-Humayma

According to the Byzantine writer Uranios, the earliest town on this site was built in obedience to an oracle consulted by King Obodas I (*c.* 96-86 BC). But it was Obodas' son, Aretas III, who founded the town, at a time when the Nabataeans were defining their territory, and a more settled population was desirable. Uranios called it Auara (Arabic: *huwara*, white); today it is al-Humayma, lying in Wadi Hisma in southern Jordan.

While Auara clearly filled a provisioning and security gap in the trade route south of Petra, a major drawback was its total lack of water. But if a settlement was needed at just that point, the Nabataean attitude was that water could be caught or brought. Numerous reservoirs were dug to catch run-off water during winter rains, and 27km of covered aqueducts channelled water from springs in the Shara mountains just to the north. This water supply may have encouraged local bedouin to come here for trade, and to settle for a while each year to grow crops which helped provision the trading caravans.

The Roman expansion of al-Humayma included a large rectangular fort, in AD 400 the base of locally recruited Native Horse Archers. In the early 8th century the town was the home of the Abbasid family, who built a handsome palace here. It was at al-Humayma that they plotted their rebellion against the Umayyad caliphs, ousting them in 750.

Few Nabataean remains are visible above ground at al-Humayma, where the large Roman fort dominates; the Abbasid palace is in the lower centre of the picture

Following pages: A flock of goats in the arid lands south of al-Humayma

Part 6
The South

Faynan

One of life's transforming discoveries – how to smelt copper – occurred in the Chalcolithic ('copper-stone') age, *c.* 4500-3300 BC, and copper implements such as axes and arrowheads gradually replaced flint. In Jordan, copper mining and smelting only began at the end of this period, its main centre at Faynan, about 60km south of the Dead Sea, where Wadi Dana approaches Wadi 'Araba. The exploitation of copper was not a continuous process, but occurred as the need for arms, tools and coins dictated, and was dropped in periods when demand for copper decreased.

Faynan (perhaps Biblical Punon) was one of the largest copper-producing sites on both sides of Wadi 'Araba – some scholars suggest it was the site of King Solomon's mines. There are *c.* 250 mines in the area, and up to 200,000 tonnes of slag from different periods, which produced about 20,000 tonnes of copper.

The Romans restarted mining – probably to mint coins to pay the army – and built a town here called Phaino. The mines and kilns were mainly worked by slaves but, according to Eusebius (the 4th-century historian and bishop of Caesarea), in times of persecution Christians were sent to work here and many died in the terrible conditions. Later Phaino had its own bishop. Copper production continued here periodically up to early Mamluk times.

Previous pages: Wadi Ramm, the main wadi of the vast system that takes its name, with the village of Ramm in the middle

Faynan has been exploited for its copper since the late 4th millennium BC; the ruins of Khirbet Faynan (lower left) are mainly Roman and Byzantine

Dana

The little village of Dana perches on a shelf of the mountainside that drops down into the Wadi 'Araba rift. The single approach road ends at the beginning of the village, and from there narrow paths — some barely wide enough to walk in — run between the houses, whose flat roofs provide an easy venue for social communication. Built of stone and wood, and plastered with mud, the houses blend perfectly with the landscape.

The site has been occupied since ancient times, settlers drawn here because of its three abundant springs and good grazing. The springs still water the carefully made terraces on the hillsides, which are filled with all manner of fruits and vegetables.

The village we see today is of Ottoman origin, its houses recurrently restored to keep them habitable. But by the 1980s Dana had virtually died for many residents had moved to a new village, Qadisiyyah, by the main road on the plateau, seeking jobs at the cement factory. In the 1990s electricity was brought, and the Royal Society for the Conservation of Nature restored some houses and initiated income-generating projects — making preserves from the crops, and designing and making silver jewellery. These developments have brought many villagers back to their old houses.

When the outstandingly beautiful Dana Nature Reserve was created in the wild sandstone mountains on the other side of Wadi Dana, the villagers found more employment opportunities and became a vital part of its wildlife conservation mission.

Above: Mountains in the Dana Nature Reserve on a hazy day

Right: The single-storey, stone-built village of Dana, overlooking Wadi Dana which runs west into Wadi 'Araba

Shobak

About 25km north of Petra an imposing castle crowns a cone of rock which rises above a wild and rugged landscape. It is today named after the nearby village of Shobak; but to the Crusaders it was Crak de Montréal – the fortress of the royal mount. It was built in 1115, in the reign of Baldwin I of Jerusalem, the first of several castles designed to protect the new province of Oultrejourdain from its Muslim enemies, who attacked from the route linking Syria and Egypt – the old King's Highway.

Montréal was the base of Roman du Puy, first lord of Oultrejourdain, but in 1132 the title was given to Payan le Bouteiller, who moved to Karak ten years later. Montréal remained an important Crusader defence – it was besieged by Saladin in 1171, and again after the Crusaders' defeat at Hattin in 1187. It held out a few months longer than Karak, finally capitulating in the spring of 1189.

The Ayyubids held the castle until 1260 when the new Mamluk Sultan in Egypt, Baybars, secured the whole region under his rule. Apart from a Crusader church and chapel, and an Ayyubid palace, most of what we see today dates from a late 13th-century Mamluk restoration, including a handsome frieze of Arabic calligraphy around the outside walls. Ottoman rule lapsed into control by sheikhs of the area until the late 19th century; and the castle was inhabited by a few local families until the 1950s.

The Crusader castle at Shobak was one of the first to be built in the Province of Oultrejourdain. It was extensively rebuilt by the Mamluks

Wadi Ramm/Iram

Coming from the northern plateau, the first sight of Wadi Ramm is a bird's eye vision of crags and pinnacles thrusting up from the sandy desert floor, each stacked behind another till they dissolve in haze. This vast tract of southern Jordan takes its name from the grandest of a whole network of wadis.

'They were not unbroken walls of rock,' wrote T. E. Lawrence, in one of several lyrical passages on Wadi Ramm in *Seven Pillars of Wisdom*, 'but were built sectionally, in crags like gigantic buildings along the two sides of their street… They gave the finishing semblance of Byzantine architecture to this irresistible place: this processional way greater than imagination… Landscapes in childhood's dream were so vast and silent'. Lawrence came here during the Arab Revolt of 1917-18, when tribal politics or logistics required it, or to find solace. Much of David Lean's 1960s epic, Lawrence of Arabia, was filmed here.

Because of its springs, the area has been inhabited at least since Neolithic times. For millennia it was used by nomadic tribes, and by traders en route to or from southern Arabia; many left drawings on rock faces, or graffiti in Thamudic or Nabataean script (in which they called the area 'Iram'). A temple dedicated to the goddess Allat, built earlier by the tribe of 'Ad, was restored in the time of the Nabataean King Aretas IV; and the settlement near it dates to Rabbel II's time.

'This irresistible place: this processional way greater than imagination… Landscapes in childhood's dream were so vast and silent'. T. E. Lawrence

146

The geology of Ramm

The formations of Wadi Ramm are a spin-off from the series of cataclysms that created the Great Rift Valley, of which the Jordan rift is the deepest part. The layers of rock thrown up here were rearranged in the criss-crossing fault lines that we see today. Most run NNE-SSW but they are traversed by counter-faults in every other direction.

The valley floors lie *c.* 900-1,000m above sea level, and the sandstone crags rise a further 500-750m. Jabal Ramm (1,754m), the highest peak in the region, is the second highest in Jordan; but Jabal Umm Ishreen, facing it across the wadi, is only one metre lower.

Mostly hidden beneath the surface lies a base of pre-Cambrian granite at least 2,000 million years old. Above it are sandstones of varying ages and colours – first red Cambrian (600 million years old), with grey Ordovician above it, then pale beige Silurian – each about 100 million years younger than the one below. Rain and wind have sculpted the sandstones into forms that resemble domes, organ-pipes or dripping candle wax, and have created rock arches over canyons.

All the strata tilt down eastwards and in western areas the granite base is visible above the wadi floor. Particularly on the east face of Jabal Ramm, springs occur at the interface between granite and sandstone, caused by winter rain penetrating the porous sandstone, stopping on the impermeable granite and trickling east to form pools with lush foliage.

The granite base is visible in this photograph of the western side of the Wadi Ramm system, with sandstone of varying ages and colours above it

Above: An experimental agricultural project at ad-Disi near Wadi Ramm

Right: The Nabataean temple near the village of Ramm

Opposite: Hot air balloons compete for the Champion of Champions prize in Wadi Ramm in 1992

Aqaba

Jordan's only seaport lies half encircled by mountains at the head of the Gulf of Aqaba, an arm of the Red Sea. Its position was always strategic – as a hub of the land and sea routes linking Arabia, the Far East, Africa and Europe, and for its subterranean reserves of sweet water. It remains a busy port, and Jordan's fastest developing town.

The earliest known settlement in the area (Chalcolithic, *c.* 3500 BC) had furnaces for the smelting of copper from Wadi 'Araba. But as yet there is no clear location for Solomon's port of Ezion-geber 'near Eloth on the shore of the Red Sea, in the land of Edom' (I Ki. 9:26). It was once identified with Tell al-Khaleifeh, near the Israeli border, but the earliest finds there may be from 200 years later.

The Nabataeans founded the city of Aila within the area of present-day Aqaba, and developed it into an important trade base on the route between the Mediterranean coast and south Arabia, India and China. After the Roman annexation of AD 106 Aila's role was enhanced as the southern terminus of the new road from Bostra, the Via Nova Traiana.

Later, around 295, the city was fortified and a Roman legion based here. Excavations in recent years have uncovered a very early church of the late 3rd or early 4th century, built of mud brick. Aila's first bishop, Petros, attended the ecumenical Council at Nicaea in 325, and his successors took part in later Councils.

The port and town of Aqaba at the head of the Red Sea. The flag is that of the Arab Revolt of 1916-18

Opposite: Untouched
landscape in Wadi Hisma,
near Wadi Ramm

Left: Part of Wadi 'Araba
which runs between the
southern end of the Dead
Sea and the port of Aqaba

Below: Aqaba and the Red
Sea, seen from the granite
mountains north-east of the
town

From medieval to modern city

In the years before the Islamic conquest the Ghassanids, a Christian Arab tribe, ruled Aqaba, and in 630 their bishop — Yuhanna ibn Ru'ba — negotiated a peace treaty with the Prophet Mohammad soon after the battle of Tabuk. This ensured good relations with the new Islamic rulers — the Caliph 'Omar even stayed with the bishop on a visit in 639.

A handful of Christian carvings have been found — but few churches, probably because most of the stones were used to build the walled Islamic city and its large mosque, on a new site near the shore. Several early Islamic writers told of Aila's prosperity, both as a port and trading centre, and also as a staging post on the Hajj pilgrimage route.

By the time of the Crusades Aila was less prosperous, due to an earthquake and tribal raids. In 1116 it became part of the Latin kingdom of Jerusalem until the Crusaders

Left: The excavated Islamic city of Aila, surrounded by hotels, restaurants and the marina

Above: Aqaba's 15th-C Mamluk fort was captured from the Ottomans in 1917 during the Arab Revolt

were ousted at the end of the century. The remains of the Crusader castle here probably lie hidden beneath the 15th-century Mamluk fort near the eastern end of the gulf.

Under the Ottomans decline accelerated in 1869, for the new Suez Canal diverted many pilgrims away from the land route via Aqaba. In 1910, when Alois Musil visited, only about 19 families remained. Seven years later Aqaba was taken by an Arab and British force and the fort became a temporary base in the Arab Revolt. It was only in 1925, four years after Transjordan was founded, that Aqaba was detached from the Hijaz and became part of the new domain of Amir 'Abdullah.

Jordan timelines
Archaeological and dynastic periods

Palaeolithic period	c. 1.8 million – 16,000 BC
Epipalaeolithic (or Mesolithic) period	c. 16,000 – 8500 BC
Pre-pottery Neolithic period	c. 8500 – 5500 BC
Pottery Neolithic period	c. 5500 – 4500 BC
Chalcolithic period	c. 4500 – 3300 BC
Early Bronze Age	c. 3300 – 2000 BC
Middle Bronze Age	c. 2000 – 1550 BC
Late Bronze Age	c. 1550 – 1200 BC
Iron Age	c. 1200 – 539 BC
Assyrian period	c. 800 – 612 BC
Babylonian period	612 – 539 BC
Persian period	539 – 332 BC
Hellenistic period	332 – 63 BC
Nabataean period	312 BC – AD 106
Roman period	63 BC – AD 324
Byzantine period	AD 324 – 635
Umayyad period	635 – 750
Abbasid period	750 – 969
Fatimid period	969 – 1171
Crusader period	1099 – 1189
Ayyubid period	1171 – 1263
Mamluk period	1250 – 1516
Ottoman period	1516 – 1918

⁊

MODERN JORDAN
British mandate	1919 – 1946
Emirate of Transjordan	
Amir 'Abdullah	1921 – 1946
upgraded to Hashemite Kingdom of Jordan	
King 'Abdullah I	1946 – 1951
King Talal I	1951 – 1952
King Hussein I	1952 – 1999
King 'Abdullah II	1999 –

Index

Arabic names are listed under the actual name, not the definite article
– e.g. al-Humaymah is listed under H. Mountains are
listed under Jabal; valleys under Wadi.

The publishers wish to thank the following for their generous support
in the publication of this book:

Arab Bank
Arab International Hotels
Arab Potash Company
Aramex
Business Tourism Company
ad-Dawliyah for Hotels and Malls
Department of Antiquities (Ministry
    of Tourism)
Export & Finance Bank
Grand Hyatt Amman
Housing Bank for Trade & Finance
Inter-Continental Hotels Group
JAMCO International Plastic Company
Jordan Armed Forces
Jordan Chamber of Industry
Jordan Insurance Company
Jordan International Insurance
    Company
Jordan Investment Board

Jordan Investor Center
Jordan National Shipping Lines Company
Jordan Red Crescent
Jordan Telecom
Jordan Tourism Board
Jordinvest
JWICO (Jordan Wood Industries
    Company)
MobileCom
National Resources Investment &
    Development Corporation (Mawared)
Royal Jordanian Air Force
Salaam International Transport & Trading
    Company
Seabird Aviation Jordan
SOFEX Jordan
Steel Buildings Company
T. Gargour & Fils (Mercedes)
Union Bank